ORIGINAL PUBLICATIONS'
COMPLETE BOOK OF BATHS

By Robert Laremy

Featuring Baths for
Love, Money, Health, Happiness, Spiritual Growth,
Psychic Defense, and Fighting Bad Habits

2007
ORIGINAL PUBLICATIONS
NEW YORK

ORIGINAL PUBLICATIONS'
COMPLETE BOOK OF BATHS

© 2002 ORIGINAL PUBLICATIONS

ISBN: 978-0-942272-73-4

Original Publications
P.O. Box 236
Old Bethpage, New York 11804-0236

1-888-OCCULT-1

Printed in the United States of America

TABLE OF CONTENTS

INTRODUCTION

Water is in itself a holy liquid. Without it, no form of life can survive. The use of water as not only a physical cleanser, but a metaphysical one, is a cross-cultural phenomenon, From the Javanese custom of blessing an expectant mother with a ritual bath when she reaches her seventh month of pregnancy [the miltoni bath], to the Jewish custom called the mikveh 1, ritual bathing is truly global. In India, millions of pilgrims make the trek to the holy waters of the river Ganges, many going there to die, thus assuring themselves of a propitious death and liberation through rebirth, Two thousand years ago John the Baptist was performing mass ritual baths, when his cousin Jesus underwent the treatment, the history of the world was forever changed.

While many of these ancient rituals involved going to a natural body of water, urbanization has curtailed modern man and woman's ability to do so; our bathtubs have become our rivers and seashores! In fact, in African Diasporic religions, many rituals that called for the initiate to be taken to a river have been changed to the neophyte being taken to the bathroom. The running water that flows through metal pipes becomes a perfectly acceptable substitute for natural sources of Water. For centuries, in almost every culture, bathing has been a sacred ritual used to improve health, rejuvenate tired bodies, diminish stress and, of course, cleanse andbeautify, A bath can be anything you want it to be; a time of birth and rebirth, a purification of the soul, or a chance to pamper yourself in an ultimate relaxed state.

A powerful practitioner can perform an exorcism using only her . or his spiritual strength and water! Most of us have experienced the great relief a simple bath can offer; add to your bath water the intangible power of your intention, plus one or several of the tangible psychic protectors available, and you have at your disposal an invaluable ally in your battle against energy vampires, bad vibrations, and all sorts of spiritual maladies. Holy water, spring water, sea water, and water from a sacred source such as the River Jordan can be added to your regular bath water for protection. Salt, baking soda, camphor, Florida water, white rose petals, and an egg (make sure it doesn't break) are also powerful protectors you can add to your bath water. Before you enter the bathtub, however, take some water out and save it to use as a floor and wall wash to protect your home.

It is important when taking a spiritual bath to understand that it is different from a regular bath. A normal bath is a necessary sanitary function that removes the dirt and grime of daily living, a spiritual or ritual bath has a totally different aim, to remove unwanted energies and baleful vibrations. The act of undertaking a spiritual bath indicates that the person doing it is a believer in the higher truths. This belief in itself triggers the necessary energies that, mixed with the physical attributes of the ingredients chosen, facilitates the elimination of the unwanted vibrations and the acquisition of positive energies.

Since the spiritual bath is not intended to remove physical dirt, I advise that before taking a spiritual bath you take a good shower to remove all physical dirt, that way you can forget about washing behind the ears etc., during your ritual bath, and you can just concentrate on the spiritual aspects of your bath. Although botanicas and other stores that carry spiritual and religious supplies sell prepared baths, I strongly recommend you prepare your own, following the recipes given here, using fresh ingredients whenever possible.

The most ancient use of ritual baths, such as the Hebrew mikveh, which is 5,000 years old, involves the use of pure water, usually running water, and the recitation of a magical formula -the words empowering the water. In the Bible, it is said that "Nevertheless a fountain or pit, wherein there is plenty of water, shall be clean " (Ach Ma yan U'bor Mikveh Mayim yihyeh tahorJ Leviticus 1 1:36

Later on the Egyptians, Greeks, Romans, and many others used decoctions made from water to which minerals, herbs, roots, and tree barks had been added. In many sub-Saharan Traditional African beliefs, Herbal baths are often used when sickness is present, A common African belief is that a person can be affected through his/her roottracks, the tracks left behind by his/her footprints. This necessitates that, not only the person, but their doorstep and yard also receive periodic washings with spiritual cleansers in order to remove harmful materials such as Goofer Dust or War Water, which may had been laid down in one's path by an enemy, Bath water set aside to use in this fashion is known as a floor wash (more on floor washes later).

METHODS OF PREPARING THE BATHS

The method I prefer is to simply toss ingredients into the bathtub while it is filling with warm water. It is an easy and natural way to prepare a spiritual bath. Unfortunately, modern plumbing and drainage was not designed to accommodate large debris such as herbs, flowers, and tree barks. Tying the herbs, or placing bulky ingredients inside a bag made of tulle, gauze, or other suitable material can work. Having a good filter in the drain that can catch the larger items can also work. Some procedures call for the remains of the bath to be gathered and either be kept for further work, such as the fashioning of a mojo bag, or these remains may have to be discarded or buried, as in some baths originating in the Yoruba and Santeria traditions.

Many baths prepared by African-American practitioners involve initially boiling the ingredients in water, then letting them simmer for awhile, and finally using only the liquid for the baths. Mexican American practitioners usually use fresh herbs and do not boil their ingredients. Some like to leave ingredients in water by the sun's light to allow the herbs to `give what they want, without being forced." I use all of these methods, depending on the particular situation. My favorite is to use fresh ingredients and put them right in the bathtub as it is filling with water.

When bathing in a tub, the general rule is that warm or hot water is used to maximize relaxation, and cool water is used to energize the body. The temperature of a bath should usually be moderate, between 95° and 98°. If it is too hot, over 100°, it will drain your energy and dry your skin by removing protective oils. A very hot bath can even be dangerous, especially for someone with heart problems. Conversely, if the water is too cool, under 75°, it can depress the body's circulation and also be dangerous, especially after exercising or for people with high blood pressure.

Suggested soaking time is 5 to 20 minutes. Immersion for longer than 30 minutes can leave your skin dry and itchy, as the long soak actually leeches moisture from your skin. Care should be taken to follow some basic procedures that will maximize your benefit when undertaking a spiritual bath. After adding the necessary ingredient(s) to the bath, which should be lukewarm, immerse your nude body totally in the water. Make sure your head is totally immersed, for this is the part of your body that serves as the seat of most energies, including the ones you want to get rid of 3. Ahead I will list some widely-used baths that have been time tested and proven to work, While some New Age writers recommend that people experiment and mix ingredients according to their whim, I strongly advise against this practice. Generally speaking, tried and true baths have the advantage of having been tested over years and are more apt to work than new experimentations, Also, an inexperienced person may, without realizing it, mix ingredients that do not go well together, think of an inexperienced pharmacist giving you two drugs that have a dangerous interaction. People in the West do not show the same respect for spiritual practitioners that they show for scientists. In more ancient societies, however, especially those that have retained a close kinship to Mother Earth, the spiritual practitioner is accorded either equal or better treatment as that given to a physician. In this understanding of the importance of keeping a balance between spiritual and physical health, indigenous people are light years ahead of the so-called "modern" civilizations.

BATH INDEX

1

SOME TRIED AND TRUE BATHS

We begin this section with some of the most effective baths known to spiritual practitioners. These are recipes that have consistently given wonderful results, thus their pride of place among all baths. I have chosen the six most frequent reasons people come seeking aid, and have recorded the five most efficacious baths known to me in each category. These six categories are:

1) Removing negativity
2) Increasing one's wealth
3) Uncrossing or removing hexes and curses
4) Love problems
5) Increase of good luck
6) Maintaining good health.

BATHS TO REMOVE NEGATIVITY

In a way, successfully removing negativity is the most important action a spiritual practitioner can effectuate, for where there is no negativity, nothing deleterious can survive, thus the absence of negativity is conducive to activities that make a person productive and economically sound; lack of negativity also indicates that there is no hex or curse present, therefore no uncrossing agent is needed under such circumstances. The absence of negativity also breeds situations where love can easily grow. A lack of negativity can be thought of as having good luck! Finally, illness is synonymous with negativity, so eliminating negativity also tends to promote perfect health. Here are the five best baths for removing negativity.

ANTI-NEGATIVITY BATH #1

- *8 ounces of holy water*
- *Petals from eight white roses*
- *½ cup of Epsom salts.*

Add ingredients to half tub of lukewarm water, light white candle inside bathroom. Concentrate on ridding yourself of all negativity. After about twenty minutes, come out of the bath and pat yourself dry with a clean, white towel.

ANTI-NEGATIVITY BATH #2

- *1 cup sea water*
- *1 tablespoon ammonia*
- *1 teaspoon Epsom salts*

Warning: Do not take this bath if your skin is sensitive to ammonia.

This bath has been in use in the Middle East, with slight varia tions, since at least the 1300's. Millions of people have received benefit from it.

ANTI-NEGATIVITY BATH #3

- *1 cup milk*
- *1 teaspoon sea salt*
- *Bunch of parsley*

While this bath has been used to bring good luck, its original design was to rid person of negative energies. Goat's milk works better than cow's milk.

ANTI-NEGATIVITY BATH #4

- *1 cup Epsom salts*
- *1 teaspoon baking soda*
- *1 cup river water*

Mix all ingredients with your bath water, keep a yellow candle going while you bathe.

ANTI-NEGATIVITY BATH #5

This bath is the one most Caribbean Spiritualists prefer for getting rid of bad vibrations.

- *About 3 ounces of Florida water.*
- *1 lump of cascarilla (powdered eggshell)*
- *Petals from five white carnations*

After taking bath, take remains of petals and cascarilla and discard far from your home, for it is thought that the negativity has been absorbed by these physical remains.

BATHS TO INCREASE YOUR WEALTH

WEALTH-INCREASING BATH #1

- *2 loadstones*
- *1 clear quartz*
- *1 whole egg, cracked.*

Add everything to your bath water, bathe for thirty minutes.

WEALTH-INCREASING BATH #2

- *1 bunch of parsley*
- *1 cup of goat's milk*
- *1 stick of cinnamon*

Add everything to your bath water, remain in tub for half an hour.

WEALTH-INCREASING BATH #3

- *Two loadstones*
- *1 ounce myrrh*
- *2 teaspoons of olive oil*

Mix all ingredients with bath water, carve a dollar sign into a green pull-out candle, dress candle with money-drawing oil, lucky 7 oil, or olive oil. Light candle while bathing, snuff out candle and re-light the next day - do this for seven consecutive days.

WEALTH-INCREASING BATH #4

- *Cut three dollar bills up in little pieces, add pieces to bath water*
- *7 pennies*
- *1 ounce of myrrh*

Add everything to your bath water,
remain in tub for half an hour.

WEALTH-INCREASING BATH #5

- *2 bunches of parsley*
- *1 bunch of rosemary*
- *5 sticks of cinnamon*

Add ingredients to very hot bath water, allow to cool down to comfortable temperature, proceed to take bath.

UNCROSSING BATHS

UNCROSSING BATH #1

Calinda Unhexing Bath

- *1 head of garlic*
- *3 leaves of sage*
- *Some geranium water*
- *Some dry basil*
- *1 bunch of parsley*
- *1 teaspoon saltpeter*

Add all ingredients to very hot bath water, allow to cool off to comfortable temperature. Do this on Monday, Wednesday, and

Friday. Rub your body with Bay Rum and vervain oil and honeysuckle afterwards. No evil thing can penetrate one who has bathed in the Calinda Unhexing Bath.

UNCROSSING BATH #2

A Wiccan uncrossing bath courtesy of
Lady Isis, HPS, Queens, New York.

1. To a clean tub, add very warm water.

2. Pour three cups of sea salt into the water, for three is a magical number, the number of Eleggua in Santería, the three aspects of the goddess (maiden, lady, crone), the Holy trinity of Christianity, the trimurti of Hinduism, and so on.

3. With your power hand (most often your power hand is the hand you write with), stir the water until the salt is dissolved and/or it feels right to you. Keeping your power hand in the water, say the following incantation:

   "Water and Earth, Blessings on thee. I cast all evil far
   from me, by the powers of the Old Ones,
   as I will, so mote it be!".

4. Standing next to the tub, facing east, say *'Lady and Lord, Goddess and God, please receive me, body and soul'* Dip your forefinger and middle finger into the water and anoint your third eye.

5. Now get into the tub and enjoy a relaxing bath, letting all your negativity dissolve in the sacred salts that surround you!

UNCROSSING BATH #3

Alabama Uncrossing Bath (Alabama Slamma)

• *9 teaspoonfuls of cooking oil.*
• *1 ounce of saltpeter.*
• *8 quarts water*

After using, you must not throw water away, for you need to use the same water a total of nine times. Never rub upwards - always run from the neck down. The last time you use that water, take it and throw it towards the sunrise, wishing the hex to go back to the woman or man who sent it.

UNCROSSING BATH #4

---

1. Read Psalm 1 before you enter bathroom.

2. Add one ounce of powdered Little John Chew to warm bath while water is running.

3. Get in and out of bath water within three minutes.

4. Read Psalm 4 as soon as you are out of the bathroom. You will feel all negativity lifted from your soul!

UNCROSSING BATH #5

Add three drops of camphor oil, three drops of eucalyptus oil, and three drops of your own urine to an early morning bath. The water should not be hot, but merely room temperature. This ancient combination rids the bather of all jinxes.

LOVE BATHS

LOVE BATH #1

- *1 ounce powdered damiana*
- *1 yellow rose (petals only)*
- *1 bunch of fresh mint*

Boil all ingredients in one quart of water until half the liquid has evaporated. Allow to cool down to room temperature, add liquid only to your bath water.

LOVE BATH #2

(This bath, from Santería, is performed under the blessings of the goddess Oshún-R.L.)

- *Five yellow roses, petals only.*
- *Five cinnamon sticks.*
- *Five different colognes (five drops from each).*
- *Five drops of honey*
- *Five drops of Florida Water.*

Of all the cleansings I have recommended in my thirty-eight years as a spiritual practitioner, I can unequivocally state that this is the one that has been most consistently successful. While some people who have done it have told me that this cleansing has literally changed their lives, no one has ever reported any negative effects from it; actually, the most common remark I've heard is "I feel so much better after having taken the Oshún baths!" It is important that the instructions be followed to the letter.

1. On a Tuesday evening, mix all ingredients on a pail of water.

2. Place pail by a window where the first light of Wednesday morning will hit it.

3. After the Sun's rays have touched the water with all of the ingredients, you are ready to add to your bath water.

4. Light a yellow candle and settle into your bath, relaxing for at least twenty minutes, asking Oshún to grant your wishes.

Do this every Wednesday for five weeks in a row. You'll be amazed at the results. This bath not only makes the person taking it more attractive all-around, it also brings good fortune and good health!

LOVE BATH #3

• *5 whole yellow oranges*

A much simpler Oshún bath for attracting lovers involves bathing with five whole oranges floating in your bath water. Play with them, pass them all over your body as you ask Oshún for a mate! Afterwards, make juice from oranges and give to a person you are attracted to, if you have that opportunity.

LOVE BATH #4

- *1 bunch of parsley*
- *5 cinnamon sticks*
- *3 red roses*

Add to very hot bath water , allow water to cool down to comfortable level, bathe for at least 20 minutes. Discard remains of bath outside your home.

LOVE BATH #5

- *1 drop of Come-To-Me oil*
- *1 drop of attraction oil.*
- *1 drop of cinnamon oil*
- *1 drop of vanilla extract*
- *1 drop of honey*
- *1 splash of Florida water*

Mix all ingredients with your bath water, remain in tub for half an hour.

GOOD-LUCK BATHS

GOOD LUCK BATH #1

Gambler's Gold Lucky 7 Bath
Attributed to legendary
New Orleans Voodoo queen Marie Laveau

- *1 ounce golden Chamomile flowers (dried)*
- *5 Cinnamon sticks.*
- *1 ounce Irish Moss.*
- *1 ounce Alfalfa.*
- *1 leaf of Five-finger-grass.*
- *1 Bay leaf*
- *1 sprig of Rosemary.*

Steep herbs for 7 minutes in boiling water. Add to bath water, sit in tub and, using a pot, Pour the bath water over your head 7 times, reciting the 23rd Psalm each time. Do this 7 days in a row.

GOOD LUCK BATH #2

"Gypsy" good-luck bath, *popularized in southern Spain in the 17th century.*

- *1 bay leaf.*
- *1 sprig of rosemary.*
- *Some holy water*

1. Boil bay leaf and rosemary in tap water for several minutes, add to bath water, then add holy water to tub.

2. Before entering the tub, say:

"House of Jerusalem, where the Christ was born, as I enter thee, clear my soul of sin, allowing goodness to enter."

3. After you enter the water, say: *"Laurel, laurel, cleanse my soul, rosemary, with gold fill my bowl. Health and wealth will come, not go. Holy water, keep me well, from all evil sortilege"*

4. Sit in the tub, relaxing, for several minutes, until you feel you can get up and leave.

GOOD LUCK BATH #3

- *1 cup of fresh strawberries*
- *7 green grapes*
- *5 golden oranges*

Put all ingredients in bath, sit in tub and play with fruit, passing them over your body. Throw out fruit far from home after bath. This bath brings good luck, keeps away evil spirits, and also attracts wealth.

GOOD LUCK BATH #4

New Orleans "Jazzman's Trick,"
popularized by Dr. John.

- *1 drop of morning, first-rise, midstream urine*
- *12 slugs*
- *A splash of your favorite cologne*

Put all ingredients in slightly warm bath water, stay in tub for at least eight minutes while chanting *"je vais ganer au joeoux ce soir, je vais ganer l'amour pertant,"* an old Creole phrase meaning *"I'll win at games of chance tonight, I'll win at games of love in time."*

GOOD LUCK BATH #5

Rose of Jericho Bath

- *1 Rose of Jericho.*
- *1 Pack of Attraction Powder [1 Oz]*
- *1 sprig of Parsley*

Draw a lukewarm bath at 7:00 AM, add all ingredients to the water. At 9:00 AM take bath (do not add any water, take bath at whatever temperature it is). Save Rose of Jericho on a bowl with water, add pennies to it, as well as laundry blueing.

CURATIVE BATHS

These baths have been used to cure minor illnesses, to make people feel better physically, and to restore health since time immemorial.

CURATIVE BATH #1

- *1 ounce dried Betony*
- *1 cup Epsom salts*
- *1 solid 2" square Camphor tablet*

Add everything to your bath water, relax in the curative warmth of your bath until you feel strengthened and restored to good health, approximately 45 minutes.

CURATIVE BATH #2

This bath is said to have saved many from different outbursts of plagues.

- *4 ounces of Four Thieves Vinegar*
- *Petals from 4 Pansies*
- *2" square solid Camphor*

Place camphor and petals inside bathtub before adding water. After filling the bathtub half way, add vinegar. Get in and finish filling bathtub with water as warm as you can stand it without getting burned. Repeat bath three more times, leaving a day in between each bath.

CURATIVE BATH #3

If you are feeling weak, anemic, add ½ a cup of War Water [see recipe on page —] to your bath once per week. **Do not use War Water more than once a week as this ingredient is extremely strong.**

CURATIVE BATH #4

- *7 drops Violet oil.*
- *7 drops Hyssop oil.*
- *7 drops Camphor oil.*

Mix all ingredients with bath water. Light purple candle while bathing. Repeat seven days in a row. Will heal many physical, mental, and emotional maladies.

2

HERBS TO USE IN YOUR BATHS

The use of herbs in ritual baths is a tradition that goes back thousands of years. Psalm 51 in the Bible mentions the use of hyssop in a ritual bath to get rid of sin. Different herbs are ascribed different powers. Mostly, herbs are thought to aid in love-getting, money-drawing, protection from evil, or the removal of curses. The method of preparation varies. In North America, most root doctors recommend that you steep the herbs in boiling water, strain the mixture, let the liquid cool, and pour it over your body while standing in a wash tub. This is the most traditional way of taking an herbal bath. Many root doctors tell their clients to pour the bath water over their heads a specified number of times (invariably an odd number) and some also prescribe the reciting of Psalms or magical phrases as the water is poured. The reason for this particular posture - standing, rather than sitting or laying down - reflects the reality that most clients of root doctors didn't have the luxury of a bathtub! Had they enjoyed such amenities, I'm sure the recommendation would have been to pour the liquid into a warm bath and relax in it a few minutes!

The used bath water, enhanced by the essence of the bather, is very often an ingredient in floor washes in the Hoodoo tradition (though not so in Santería, where the pre-used water is preferred). The commonly-encountered recommendation to use only spring water, river water, or ocean water in preparing spiritual baths is similar to the Jewish-Kabbalist custom of using free running water in the ritual bath menstruating women must take.

HERBAL HAND WASHES

A gambler's hands are his principal weapons, this is particularly true of those who play cards and throw dice. The same money-drawing herbs used for ritual bathing may be used to fashion lucky hand washes. These are used for cleaning and empowering the hands when going out to play at games of chance. A typical product of this type is Gambler's Gold Lucky 7 Hand Wash, which should contain golden Chamomile, money-drawing Cinnamon Chips, money steadying Irish Moss, poverty-ending Alfalfa, Five-Finger Grass, Bay Leaves, and Rosemary.

There is no way of knowing if pre-packaged products actually contain the necessary herbs, but a good practice, if you must buy commercially-prepared baths, hand washes, and floor washes, is to go with brands that have been around a long time and are recommended by established botanicas and stores (at the end of this book we'll provide a list of reputable suppliers). To make an herbal hand wash, the practitioner makes up a batch as a strong "tea," strains out the herbs, and stores the liquid in the refrigerator, using just enough every time to thoroughly wash the hands and prepare them for their work.

Alfalfa - Add to your bath water to make you wealthy.

Almond - Unites lovers; excellent for two lovers to bathe together.

Allspice - Increases the "Love" vibrations in a generalized way.

Aloe - Enormously popular in Semitic societies, the aloe plant has strong associations with Muhammad. It is said to bring success, love, and protection to the user.

Angelica - Brings peace and angelic vibrations. Belongs to St. Michael the Archangel.

Anise - Brings love, pleasant dreams, and youthful vigor to wearer.

Balm of Gilead - Romans added it to their baths as an aphrodisiac.

Basil - Attracts high vibrations; fills your aura with positive energy, antithetical to the negativity caused by energy vampires. Add Florida Water to the bath for maximum benefit.

Bayberry - Attracts money.

Bay leaves (LAUREL) - Makes you immune to psychic attacks. You should also light a white candle in the bathroom while taking the bath. Read 83rd Psalm before entering water for maximum effect.

Betony - Restores physical health; keeps away evil spirits.

Blackberry - Powerful ingredient in baths to repel evil.

Blessed Thistle - Used to invoke the god Pan and as an aphrodisiac.

Bloodroot - Protects against hexes; uncrossing agent. *Use only in tiny amounts, as it can be highly toxic.*

Caraway - Initiatory baths usually include this plant as an ingredient. It brings good luck to newlyweds.

Catnip - Calms and blesses the bather.

Cayenne - Induces sobriety.

Cedar - Attracts money.

Calendula - Conducive to peaceful sleep; makes your dreams come true.

Calamus Root - Use when you want to attract attention.

Chamomile Flowers - Draw money and love. Ancient Romans used Chamomile as an eye wash to relieve ocular strain.

Cinnamon Sticks - For love and gambling luck.

Cinquefoil - Keeps away evil entities. Was one of the ingredients in witchcraft's famous flying ointment.

Clover - Repels evil spirits.

Cloves - Bring peace to the home. Gives you power over others.

Coltsfoot - A healing herb.

Comfrey Root - Insures your physical safety while you travel.

Damiana - Add to your bath water to bring sex to your life.

Dandelion - Makes wishes come true.

Dill - Improves your general health when added to bath water.

Dragon's Blood Reed - Add to your bath water to help you solve legal problems.

Elder - A powerful herb of divination and protection from all sorts of evil.

Elecampagne - An herb of initiation and psychic protection.

Eucalyptus - Helps to get rid of bad habits or evil companions.

Fennel - Protects from hexes. Gives sexual power.

Galangal root - Add to your bath to win a court case.

Garlic - Protects against energy vampires and evil spirits.

High John the Conqueror Root - For money or sex, depending how it is worked.

Honeysuckle - For love and good fortune.

Hops - Cures insomnia.

Hyacinth - Add to any love bath and it makes it work for gay men.

Hyssop - Perhaps the most well-known bath-herb in the African-American Christian community is Hyssop, mentioned in Psalm 51 of the Bible as the herb to use for purification from sin. Very strong "stripper" of bad energies, should be used with care in baths, but works very well in floor washes. For baths, use only a small quantity and do not stay in the bathtub more than eight minutes, for hyssop can cause headaches if too much of it is used for too long a time.

Irish Moss - Brings good fortune.

Jasmine - Acts as an aphrodisiac.

Lavender - Brings a high vibratory frequency to your psyche; increases your psychic powers.

Lemongrass - Brings love to your life.

Lettuce - Brings clarity and calm.

Lemon Balm - Brings love to your life.

Little John Chew - Add a little to your regular bath water to unhex any minor curse you may be experiencing. It also brings general good fortune.

Low John the Conqueror Root - Add to your bath water to attract wealth.

Mandrake - Aphrodisiac; psychic enhancer; uncrossing.

Marigold - Natives of Mexico use it as a visionary aid.

Mint - Brings a sweet, happy, vibration. Also, a mild aphrodisiac. May not be strong enough for serious energy-depleting attacks. Use as a floor wash before parties to ensure peace and joy.

Mistletoe - An aphrodisiac.

Nettles - Albertus Magnus recommended using oil of this plant with oil of houseleek to attract fish.

Nutmeg - Add three to your bathwater to bring you luck in games of chance and the stock market.

Orris - Brings peace.

Queen of the Meadow - Long a favorite bath additive, it brings good luck.

Patchouli - Protection; uncrossing.

Parsley - Great for attracting wealth. With milk, it also serves as a spiritual restorative. May not be strong enough to fight a very powerful vampire.

Purslane - Brings money and the protection of the Mother Goddess.

Raspberry Leaves - Increases a woman's attractiveness.

Rose Petals (WHITE) - Excellent bath to keep your aura strong. Eight roses are needed to provide the necessary strength to fight a vampire. Even if you do not feel you are under attack, take this bath once per week, on Thursdays, as a preventive measure.

Rosemary - Brings good fortune, but may not be strong enough by itself to stave off an energy vampire's attack. Mix with bay leaves.

Rue - Gather the rue in front of you, by your altar (if you have one). Light a purple candle and, putting your hands over the rue, palms touching the herb, say:

"In the name of God the Father, his power the Shekinnah, and their offspring the Christ, I compel this rue to be ruth, eliminating the ruthless. By the secret name of God, Adonai-Eloim-Yaweh-Amen."

Use some in your baths and floor washes to keep evil away.

Saint John's Wort - An herb of protection dating back to the early Greeks; an effective anti-depressant, even as a bath.

Sage - Works better burned than in baths. Use in baths if specifically told to do so by a spiritual practitioner, or if you were told to do so in a dream. It increases your wisdom.

Sea Lettuce - Keep some in a jar full of alcohol, then use a bit of the alcohol in your bath to bring you peace of mind and good luck.

Slippery Elm - Adding it to your bathwater keeps people from gossiping about you.

Snake Root - Boil a handful for fifteen minutes, then throw away solids and keep liquid in a bottle for seven days, on the eighth day, add it to your bathwater to make you attract wealth.

Thyme - Attracts good spirits, uncrosses.

Valerian - Purifies the aura.

Vervain - Excellent for keeping away psychic attacks.

Violet - Fresh, dried, or its oil. Brings good spirits, heals the body.

Willow - In Europe, an herb of eloquence; in China, a source of magical protection.

Witch Hazel - In Santería , a cleansing herb.

Wormwood - Fry some wormwood powder in butter, add a pinch to your bathwater as a protector against curses.

Yarrow - This herb is said to increase the human potential for expressing and understanding love.

3

PSALMS AND YOUR BATHS

Psalms have been identified with ritual baths for thousands of years. It was in the Psalms that King David said "Purge me with hyssop, and I shall be clean: Wash me, and I shall be whiter than snow." (Psalm 51:7) In my book *The Psalm Workbook* (Plainview, New York: Original Publications, 2001) I explain in detail what each Psalm can be magically used for. In Italy, Spain, and other countries of Latin origins, this practice is quite common. It is called "ensalmar" in Spanish. The practice is increasing as the magical properties of the Psalms become less the property of hermetic Kabbalists and more accessible to all who need help. Among my teachers were the noted Kabbalists Rabbi William Heim and Rabbi Jacob Neusner, the most prolific academic writer in the world. For best results, adhere to the method here described without deviation.

Firstly, do not attempt to address many problems at once. Concentrate on one problem at a time and you'll achieve better results.

Look in my book *The Psalm Workbook,* or in the list I offer at the end of this chapter, for the Psalm that addresses the problem you are taking on. Then, know that each day for seven consecutive days you will be taking a ritual bath at the same approximate time.

During this seven-day period, read Psalm 3 as soon as you wake up in the morning and read Psalm 4 before going to sleep at night.

As water rushes out of the spigot, filling the tub, reverently read the selected Psalm, then get into the water and meditate on the condition you need to remedy. If in my Psalm book I advise to add something to the bath, such as an herb or a mineral, do so before you get in the tub. It is also a good idea to have a candle lit while you are ridding yourself of a negative condition or working to attract good vibrations. The reason for doing this during the seven-day period of your cleansing is that lighting a candle and then putting it out when the ceremony is through lets the universe know the ritual has concluded, and you may go on to scrub, soap, and rinse as you would in a "regular" bath.

The key to working with Psalms is the attitude you take. For best results, bring a strong, positive demeanor to the equation. Trust that God can and WILL remedy your situation. A prayerful heart, a clear conscience, and a contrite spirit, can bring balance to a suppliant's life. After the bath, keep on exhibiting a positive attitude. Wear your favorite cologne, dress in impeccable clothes, make sure you are well groomed - many times depressed people forget to make themselves presentable, yet this is precisely where they must put their best face forward.

SELECTED SPECIFIC BATHS USING PSALMS

Psalm 132: To acquire material wealth.

Fill bathtub with warm water; add seven bunches of parsley. While relaxing in bathtub, read verses 12 through 18 with conviction. An increase in wealth will soon be noted.

Psalm 91: Simple yet effective uncrossing bath.

One deceptively simple yet organically potent bath that you cantake to remove hexes and curses sent your way is to put three teaspoons of sea salt in your bathwater and repeat the Psalm 91 seven times as you soak. This powerful yet uncomplicated procedure has proven very effective over the years.

PROBLEM / SITUATION	PSALM
Achieve prominence as a performer	87
Acquiring wealth	92, 132
Addictions	101, 124
Anxiety	138
Attracting a lover	88
Blessing a new home	61
Court cases	4, 7, 68, 99, 86
Decision making	23
Defeat enemies	1, 3, 48, 79, 94, 112, 145
Demons	118
Depression	90, 117
Domination	84
Dreams	42, 96
Drunkenness	37, 107
Employment	88, 111, 120, 123
Evil Spirits	10, 29
Exorcism	38
Eye trouble	6
Families	27, 96, 128, 133
Fear	3
Fertility	102
Fevers	105, 106
Good Luck	21

4

THREE-INGREDIENTS
AND SEVEN-INGREDIENTS BATHS

The Voodoo tradition of New Orleans reached its golden age in the middle part of the last century under the leadership of a wise and powerful woman named Marie Laveau, who systematized the religion and wrote down most of its spells, incantations, and directions for making talismans and for preparing different kinds of spiritual baths. According to Marie Laveau, the best numbers to work with are three and seven. Based on this belief, she designed a number of baths which had either three or seven ingredients each. Here are some of the baths she and some of her contemporaries designed.

TO ATTRACT WEALTH

- *4 ounces of oil of bergamot*
- *4 ounces bicarbonate of soda*
- *1 teaspoon saltpeter*

1. Take a white taper candle, break it in half, light the bottom half (throw the top half away). Let the candle burn itself out.

2. Make a wish.
3. Mix all ingredients with your bathwater using your right hand. Take bath.
4. After bath, take a little brimstone (sulfur) and burn it, throw some sugar on it. Burn brimstone and sugar Monday, Wednesday and Friday, each time making wish.

ANOTHER ONE TO ATTRACT WEALTH

• *1 ounce Saltpeter*
• *1 teaspoon brown sugar*
• *1 teaspoon powdered bluestone (substitute blueing laundry aid in place of the highly toxic bluestone)*

For success in business, mix ingredients with your bathwater once per week.

STILL ANOTHER BATH TO ATTRACT WEALTH
(you can't have too many!)

• *¼ teaspoon sulfur*
• *1 teaspoon brown sugar*
• *1 bunch of parsley*

Mix all ingredients with your bathwater.

THREE-INGREDIENTS LOVE BATH

- *3 ounces sandalwood oil*
- *3 ounces oil of Cloves*
- *I splash Orange Blossom oil*

Add all ingredients to your bathwater at dusk, get in tub, recite the following poem while standing in the tub, holding a white lighted candle.

> *Nymphs of water, sprites of air, bring me some-one nice who cares, I don't want a screaming ninny, not too fat, and not too skinny. Make him have a heart of gold, and in bed he won't be cold. Let him serve me to a tee, as I will, so mote it be!*

After bathing for at least 20 minutes, fantasizing and imagining sexual situations, go out into the world and enjoy the results of this very efficacious bath. (This is a Wiccan adaptation of an old formula).

DR. JOHN'S SEVEN INGREDIENTS LOVE BATH FOR MEN

- *1 ounce of fresh Sage*
- *1 ounce powdered Vetivert*
- *1 ounce powdered Orris root*
- *½ ounce powdered Clover*
- *1 ounce powdered Vervain*
- *1 Bay Leaf*
- *1 sprig Rosemary*

Boil everything in ½ quart water for a minute, then lower heat and simmer for ten minutes. Strain liquid into a glass jar and save, use about ½ cup for each bath. Dr. John, the famed Voodoo king from New Orleans, designed this bath for men to attract women. Martha Bishop, a spiritual advisor from Tennessee, says that if you substitute lilac for rosemary, it works for gay men to attract other gay men.

MARIE SALOPE'S SEVEN INGREDIENTS LOVE BATH FOR WOMEN

A contemporary and partner of Marie Laveau, Marie Salope was her teacher as well as her servant!

- *1 ounce rose buds.*
- *1 ounce ground orange rinds.*
- *1 sprig rosemary.*
- *1 ounce powdered myrtle.*
- *1 sprig thyme.*
- *1 drop of honey.*
- *5 sticks of cinnamon.*

Bring all ingredients to a boil in one quart of water, then allow to simmer in extremely low heat for several minutes. Strain liquid into a glass jar. Use ½ cup in each bath.

MARIE LAVEAU'S THREE INGREDIENTS PEACE BATH

"Oh, my daughter, you come to me distraught with life's problems, a husband who doesn't understand you, ten children all wanting your time. You feel cornered and tired. Well, let me tell you how all of these things will seem minor, and your own guiding spirits will lift you from your gloom. Take some linden, some lavender, and some chamomile, and rip them up a little in a pail full of water. Let the herbs stand in the water, under the rays of a good, hot, sun for as long as the day is bright. Then, at night, fill your bathtub with warm water, add the water from the pail, straining out the herbs, and relax for a good while. Fail not to do this and peace will enter your life."-

from Marie Laveau's private notebook.

CLASSIC SEVEN INGREDIENTS GOOD-LUCK BATH

* *Dragon's blood resin*
* *Colt's foot*
* *Rosemary*
* *Irish moss*
* *Bay leaves*
* *Violet*
* *Five-fingers grass*

Add a fistful of each herb to your bath water for general good luck.

THREE INGREDIENTS BATH
TO MAKE WISHES COME TRUE

* *3 drops of bergamot.*
* *1 cup baking soda.*
* *1 teaspoon saltpeter.*

Mix all ingredients with bathwater, break a taper (slender white candle) in half as you make a wish. Light the bottom half of candle. Let it burn out on its own. Repeat each Monday, Wednesday, and Friday until you are satisfied. Your wish will come true within 21 days, but remember the old adage, be very careful what you wish for, cause you just might get it!

THREE INGREDIENTS UNCROSSING BATH

- *1 cup sea salt*
- *1 cup Epsom salt*
- *1 ounce bloodroot powder*

Mix all ingredients with bathwater. Then, lay down in the water for at least twenty minutes; give it your burden. Imagine yourself rising as a new person when you are ready to leave your bath.

THREE INGREDIENTS BATH TO ATTRACT LOVE AND MONEY

- *1 ball (or square) of laundry blueing*
- *A pinch of Saltpeter*
- *½ a cup of Sugar*

Add all ingredients to very hot bathwater, wait for water to cool down to a comfortable temperature. Bathe for at least twenty minutes envisioning what you are seeking—a grand house, a strikingly handsome beau, a voluptuous señorita. If you put enough faith in what you are doing, you'll be amazed at the results.

5

ASTROLOGICAL BATHS

"Astrology represents the summation of all the psychological knowledge of antiquity"—Carl Jung

Although admittedly astrology is not my specialty, my energies having long ago been diverted to forces much nearer to our reality than the far away planets, I deeply respect this science and those who practice it with devotion, such as Enfuna Kanaga, a Dogon practitioner from Mali.. It was the Reverend Mr. Kanaga who gave me much of the information contained in this chapter. Rev. Kanaga's people have been practicing astrology for eons (although he has also been trained in western astrology). They were aware of the star Sirius long before Western astronomy confirmed its existence! Following Rev. Kanaga's suggestions, I've listed the seven herbs and/or essential oils that are most compatible with each sign. Next to the substance, I've listed what each is most potent for—love, money—If you use all seven in a bath you will be receiving generalized good fortune.

Aries [ruled by Mars] **Best day Thursday**

Allspice [L,W]
Cinnamon [L]
Cumin [W]
Clove [P]

Dragon's Blood [J]
Galangal [J]
Peppermint
[L,P,W]

Taurus [ruled by Venus] **Best day Tuesday**

Apple Blossom [L,P]
Cardamom [L,W]
Honeysuckle [L]
Patchouli [U,P,L]

Thyme [U,W]
Violet [C,W]
Rose [L]

Gemini [ruled by Mercury] **Best day Saturday**

Lavender [P,W]
Lemongrass [L]
Dill [W]
Anise [W]

Clover [U,W]
Parsley [M,L]
Peppermint [P]

Cancer [Moonchildren; ruled by the Moon] **Best day Tuesday**

Eucalyptus [U,W]
Jasmine [W,L]
Myrrh [P,W]
Lemon Balm [L]

Lilac [PA,W,L]
Gardenia [W,L]
Sandalwood [PA,L,W]

*Love [L], Money [M], Psychic Awareness [PA], Uncrossing, Protection [U],
Curative [C], Good Luck [G], Peace [P],
Justice and Court Cases [J], All-around Wellness [W].*

Leo *(ruled by the Sun)* **Best day Monday**

Benzoin [P,W]   Sandalwood [PA,L,W]
Cinnamon [L,M]   Orange [L]
Frankincense [P]   Rosemary [M,W]
Nutmeg [M]

Virgo *(ruled by Mercury)* **Best day Wednesday**

Almond [L, P]   Lavender [P]
Dill [W]   Patchouli [L,P]
Fennel [U]   Peppermint [P]
Honeysuckle [L,W]

Libra *(ruled by Venus)* **Best day Thursday**

Apple Blossom [L]   Rose [L,W,U]
Catnip [W]   Spearmint [L,P,W,C]
Marjoram [C,W,P]   Thyme [U,P,W]
Mugwort [P]

Scorpio *(ruled by Mars, Pluto)* **Best day Saturday**

Allspice [L,W]   Cumin [L]
Ambergris [U,P]   Galangal [J]
Basil [U,P]   Ginger [C,L,W]
Clove [L]

*Love **[L]**, Money **[M]**,   Psychic Awareness **[PA]**,   Uncrossing, Protection **[U]**,
Curative **[C]**, Good Luck **[G]**, Peace **[P]**,
Justice and Court Cases **[J]**, All-around Wellness **[W]**.*

Sagittarius *(ruled by Jupiter)* **Best day Friday**

Anise [U,PA]   Ginger [C,L,W]
Clove [L]   Honeysuckle [L]
Dragon's Blood [U, P]   Nutmeg [M, G, PA]
Frankincense [P]

Capricorn *(ruled by Saturn)* **Best day Monday**

Cypress [P,U]   Patchouli [L,P,W]
Honeysuckle [L]   Vervain [U, W]
Mimosa [W,PA]   Vetivert [P,W.L]
Oakmoss [M,P,W]

Aquarius *(ruled by Saturn and Uranus)* **Best day Friday**

Cypress [P,U]   Mimosa [W,PA]
Lavender [P,W]   Patchouli [P,L,U]

Pisces *(ruled by Jupiter and Neptune)* **Best day Wednesday**

Anise [L]   Nutmeg [M, G, PA]
Clove [L]   Orris [U]
Eucalyptus [C]   Sage [P]
Honeysuckle [L]

*Love [L], Money [M],   Psychic Awareness [PA],   Uncrossing, Protection [U],
Curative [C], Good Luck [G], Peace [P],
Justice and Court Cases [J],   All-around Wellness [W].*

The following baths should be taken by the appropriate person once per month.

NAME	COLOR	RECIPE	DIRECTIONS
Air Bath (Elemental) *For* **GEMINI, LIBRA, AQUARIUS**	Yellow	3 parts Lavender 2 parts Rosemary 1 part Peppermint 1 part Bergamot	*Use to access the element of Air, to improve your divinations, your memory, concentration, clear thinking, visualization and studies.*
Water Bath (Elemental) *For* **PISCES CANCER SCORPIO**	Dark Blue	2 parts Chamomile 2 parts Yarrow 1 part Ylang Ylang 1 part Palmarosa	*Use to be in harmony with the element of Water, improve intuition, bring love, increase psychic awareness, start friendships, and promote healing.*
Fire Bath (Elemental) *For* **ARIES LEO SAGITTARIUS.**	Red	3 parts Frankincense 2 parts Basil 2 parts Juniper 1/2 part Orange	*For the element of Fire. For rituals designed to bring forth strength, courage, passion, and lust.*
Earth Bath (Elemental) *For* **TAURUS VIRGO CAPRICORN.**	Green	4 parts Patchouli 3 parts Cypress 1 part Vertivert	*Use to harmonize with the element of Earth; to attract money; increase stability, augment creativity, and promote fertility.*

Hippocrates said: "a physician without a knowledge of astrology has no right to call himself a physician." Following I provide the herbs that belong to each astrological planet. To bring that planet's influence into your life, simply prepare a bath of 3, 7, or 9 of its herbs by boiling the herbs in water, then straining them out, keeping the liquid in the refrigerator. Use a cup of the liquid for each bath.

THE SUN

Appropriate to induce optimism, to help realize our goals, and to boost our sense of self-worth. Use these herbs if you are timid and scared of public speaking. The solar herbs are:

Almond	*Marigold*
Angelica	*Olive*
Ash	*St. John's Wort*
Burnet	*Sunflower*
Bay	*Vine*
Chamomile	*Walnut*
Frankincense	

THE MOON

These herbs address the emotional side of humankind. They are the herbs used in love spells and baths. They are mostly feminine and sensitive, bringing with them a childlike innocence.

Adder's Tongue	*Clary*	*Jasmine*
Anise	*Coriander*	*Lettuce*
Cabbage	*Cucumber*	*Orris*
Camphor	*Ginger*	
Chickweed	*Iris*	

MERCURY

Planet that rules the nervous system, the respiratory system, and communications.

Agaric	*Cedar*	*Hazelnut*
Azalea	*Celery*	*Lavender*
Bayberry	*Dill*	*Mace*
Bittersweet	*Fennel*	*Mulberry*
Caraway	*Fenugreek*	*Parsley*
Carrot	*Five-finger grass*	*Senna*
Cascara	*Flax*	*Valerian*

VENUS

The herbs of Venus lift the spirits of the sullen and morose. These herbs make us feel attractive, thus we become so. Contrary to popular belief, herbs of Venus should not be used to mend broken hearts—Jupiter's herbs are more appropriate for that. The herbs of Venus do act on our reproductive systems, so they serve to strengthen our libido. They also help invigorate the blood, kidneys, throat, and genitalia.

Apple blossom	*Cherry*	*Lemon balm*
Apricot	*Chick-pea*	*Lemongrass*
Bergamot	*Clover*	*Ragweed*
Birch	*Daffodil*	*Rose*
Blackberry	*Elder*	*Vervain*
Bloodroot	*Feverfew*	*Yarrow*
Burdock	*Hibiscus*	
Catnip	*Lemon*	

MARS

Herbs of Mars invigorate the sex organs, as well as the aura.

Acacia	Cumin	Marjoram
Aloe Vera	Curry	Mustard
Barberry	Fern (male plant)	Onion
Basil	Dragon's blood reed	Radish
Blessed thistle	Garlic	Rhubarb
Cashew	Honeysuckle	Tarragon
Cayenne	Horseradish	Tobacco
Chili	Juniper	Wormwood
Cubebs	Leeks	

JUPITER

The herbs belonging to Jupiter are those associated with awareness of one's needs. Also, Jupiter represents growth, both physical and spiritual. Baths of Jupiter, then, promote the magician's ability to extrapolate from the world writ small of the circle to the world writ large of the city, country, or planet; this is the mark of a good diviner.

Agrimony	Dandelion	Mistletoe
Alfalfa	Endive	Moss
Asparagus	Fig	Sandalwood
Borage	Henna	Spinach
Cardamom	Lime	Thorn apple
Chestnut	Liverwort	
Corn	Magnolia	

SATURN

Saturn is a planet of structure. Saturn rules the skeleton, ligaments, teeth, hearing, and the gall bladder. Saturn's herbs provide grounding; bathing in them helps you stay focused while involved in pursuit of the Higher Truths. Herbs of Saturn balance karma—they work well when mixed with Mercurial herbs. Use caution when working with Saturn, as this is a planet of great changes.

Amaranth	*Cypress Elm*	*Pansies*
Arnica	*Gladiolus*	*Poplar*
Barley	*Hemlock*	*Poppy*
Beets	*Hemp*	*Potato*
Belladonna	*Holly*	*Queen's delight*
Bluebell	*Irish moss*	*Skullcap*
Carob	*Ivy*	*Snakeweed*
Comfrey	*Musk*	*Wolf's bane*
Cornflower	*Nightshade*	*Yew*

URANUS

The herbs of Uranus open up the third eye. They also produce visions and prophetic dreams. Baths using these herbs increase creativity. On the physical side, Neptune works well with the organs of the body that pass fluids.

Allspice	*Elecampagne*	*Nutmeg*
Arbutus, trailing	*Gingseng*	*Pimpernel*
Chicory	*Cola nuts*	*Woody Nightshade*
Clove	*Linseed*	
Coffee	*Mandrake*	

PLUTO

A planet of the subconscious, it is also the planet of primal sexual drive, the planet of procreation instincts. Bathing in these herbs restores sexual potency and general vigor.

Agaric	*Dragon's blood*	*Rye*
Ambergris	*Eucalyptus*	*Wheat*
Asafoetida	*Hops*	*Yucca*
Cohosh	*Orchid root*	
Damiana	*Patchouli*	

6

NEW INTERPRETATIONS / ANCIENT BATHS

My associate and student Lady Isis, HPS, has been working with the more traditional baths now for over fifteen years. She has given her own twist to many of the old "tried-and-true" baths with remarkable success. Her baths seem to work especially well with young, professional women. What follows are some of her most successful recipes. Unless specified, the method used is to pour the ingredients directly in the bathwater as the tub is filling up, mixing them with your power arm (the one you write with).

LADY ISIS' AROUSING LOVE BATH

- *Petals from three red roses*
- *A sprig of rosemary*
- *A sprig of thyme*
- *Some powdered myrtle*
- *5 drops jasmine oil*
- *1 acacia flower*
- *3 drops of musk oil*

Stay in the water for at least twenty minutes. Take this bath each time you are going out to meet potential lovers.

PSYCHIC ENHANCEMENT BATH

- *3 sprigs of thyme*
- *2 ounces powdered yarrow*
- *2 white roses, petals only*
- *1 sprig of patchouli*
- *1 Nutmeg*

Bathe in this mixture to relax the conscious mind and to stimulate psychic awareness.

THIRD-EYE DEVELOPMENT BATH

- *3 ounces fresh lemongrass*
- *2 ounces fresh thyme*
- *2 ounces grated orange rind*
- *5 cloves*
- *1 part cinnamon*

Take at least once per week to stimulate development of higher functions of your psyche.

PSYCHIC DEVELOPMENT BATH

- *4 parts Yarrow*
- *1 part Bay*

Use this blend in baths to strengthen your psychic awareness.

ATTRACTION BATH

- *Patchouli leaves*
- *Lemon Vervain*
- *Cinnamon*
- *Vetivert*
- *Pink coloring*

Soak in mixture for twenty-three minutes

BATH TO ATTRACT SOULMATE

- *Petals from five pink roses*
- *2 ounces anisette liquor*
- *1 sprig of fresh dill*

Take this bath daily until your soul mate arrives.

LOVE BATH #1

- *Petals from three red roses*
- *2 geraniums*
- *1 sprig rosemary*

Let ingredients mix well with bathwater, take bath daily to keep yourself attractive.

LOVE BATH #2

- *3 sprigs of rosemary*
- *3 ounces of lavender*
- *1 ounce of cardamom*
- *1 ounce of yarrow*

Brings two sexually compatible people together.

AURA-STRENGTHENING BATH

- *3 sprigs of marjoram*
- *3 sprigs of thyme*

Use often to remain psychically strong.

ENERGY-REPLENISHING BATH

- *3 carnations, petals only.*
- *3 ounces of lavender*
- *1 sprig of rosemary*
- *1 sprig of basil*

An excellent bath to take when you feel down.

ANTI-DEPRESSION BATH

- *4 teaspoons of dried peppermint*
- *4 teaspoons of dried rosemary*
- *4 teaspoons of eucalyptus*
- *2 pine needles from a tree that's on a beach*

Mix all ingredients in scorching water—allow to cool to a temperature you can stand without getting burned, then immerse yourself in the water, allowing all your problems to go away.

ANOTHER ANTI-DEPRESSION BATH

- *3 teaspoons of dried chamomile*
- *3 teaspoons of dried lavender*
- *3 teaspoons of dried star anise*
- *3 dried sandalwood chips*

Boil mixture in water for ten minutes, then let stand for 20. Strain, add liquid to warm bathwater. Enjoy!

ANTI-DEPRESSION BATH #3

In this bath, use only fresh herbs. Tear them under the faucet as your tub is being filled. Use about a handful of each herb.

- *Chamomile*
- *Lavender*
- *Lemon balm*
- *Marjoram*
- *Sandalwood*
- *Star anise*

Relax in this soothing bath for twenty minutes, keep adding hot water so you won't feel cold.

ENERGY-RAISING BATH

- ½ Cup Lavender
- ½ Cup Rose Petals
- ½ Cup Sage
- ½ Cup Rosemary

Mix all ingredients together, gather them and tie them inside a cheesecloth. Place cheese cloth full of herbs under running water as tub gets filled. Then, relax and enjoy your bath.

HEALING BATH

- *3 sprigs of fresh rosemary.*
- *2 teaspoons of powdered or granulated lavender.*
- *2 white roses [petals only].*
- *1 sprig fresh peppermint.*
- *1 stick of cinnamon*
- *1 teaspoon eucalyptus oil.*

This bath speeds up the healing process and alleviates the symptoms of colds and flu.

UNCROSSING BATH

- *4 sprigs of rosemary.*
- *3 ounces of Juniper.*
- *2 bay leaves.*
- *1 ounce Mugwort.*

Soak all ingredients overnight, place by a window where light of the sun will hit ingredients in the morning. Take bath shortly after

ANTI-ADDICTION BATH

• *2 sprigs of rosemary.*
• *1 teaspoon granulated lavender.*
• *1 ounce of lemongrass.*
• *1 ounce of lemon vervain.*
• *1 sprig of fresh sage.*

   Place all ingredients inside a bag made of cheesecloth. Put bag in tub before you add water. Allow very hot water to fill tub. When water becomes bearable, temperature-wise, lay there visualizing your bad habit being absorbed by the water, then pull the plug and watch the water drain out, as your addiction will also leave you in the same manner. Repeat until desired goal is reached.

PEACE BATH

• *2 ounces catnip*
• *2 ounces hops*
• *1 ounce Jasmine*
• *1 ounce elder flowers*

   Bathe in this mixture and peace will follow you around.

MONEY-DRAWING BATH

• *3 ounces patchouli*
• *2 ounces basil*
• *1 stick of cinnamon*
• *1 piece of cedar*

   Brings the blessing of money.

PROTECTION/UNCROSSING BATH

- *4 sprigs rosemary.*
- *3 bay leaves.*
- *2 bunches of fresh basil.*
- *2 ounces of fennel.*
- *1 sprig of fresh dill.*

Bathe in this mixture often to keep your aura strong.

BLUE BATH

Strengthens the psyche, you can either add a little of the dried herb, or a few drops of oil in the water.

- *1 ball of laundry blueing.*
- *1 ounce vervain (if you are a female) or vertivert (for males).*
- *1 stick of cinnamon.*
- *1 sprig of peppermint.*
- *1 part galangal.*
- *A few drops Rue*

APHRODISIAC

Prolongs sexual intensity. Use approximately a handful of each ingredient, preferably fresh—but dried herbs o.k.

- *Rosemary*
- *Rose petals*
- *Jasmine flowers*
- *Thyme*

Mix all ingredients in bathwater—take bath shortly before engaging in sexual activity.

7

INDISPENSABLE RECIPES

The following recipes are extremely hard to find, since they are usually the closely guarded domain of the professional practitioner. I believe in the old adage that the good one puts out comes back tenfold, so I've never been close-fisted with my knowledge. Here, then, are some closely-guarded secret recipes.

FLORIDA WATER

Murray and Lanman, a New York company that made inexpensive after-shave lotions and other toiletries in the last century, came up with an essence that, while never attaining popularity as an after-shave, became one of the most broadly used spiritual cleansers in history: Florida Water. Today, probably 99% of those who use Florida Water do so in connection with its reputed esoteric value, rather than its purported use as a toilet water. Now manufactured by Lanman and Kemp, Florida Water hasn't changed its peculiar Victorian long-necked bottle shape and floral label—though the bottle is now more often than not made of plastic—in all these years, nor have the manufacturers changed the formula. For these reasons, I recommend that whenever possible, you use this commercially available product. I also recommend the Murray and Kemp brand over its imitators. But if you live in an area where you just can't get to the product, here is the most accurate recipe I've got for Florida Water.

Ingredients:

- *3 fluid ounces oil of bergamot*
- *1 fluid ounce oil of lavender*
- *1 fluid ounce oil of lemon*
- *1 ¼ fluid drachms oil of cloves*
- *2 ½ fluid drachms oil of cinnamon*
- *½ fluid drachms oil of neroli*
- *6 fluid ounces essence of jasmine*
- *2 fluid ounces essence of musk*
- *8 pints alcohol (preferably distilled from wine)*
- *1 pint rose water*

Mix all ingredients.
It is traditional to dye Florida Water a pale aqua-green

BRIMSTONE

Mix sulphur powder with a little bit of water, form into ¼ inch balls, allow to dry hard.

CASCARILLA

When practitioners from Africa came to the Americas during the shameful days of the slave trade, they tried to establish their practice in their new surroundings. A different geography, however brought home the reality of a different ecosystem lacking some staples found in the old continent. For healers from the west coast of Africa, one of these staples was a whitish-yellowish natural clay called mpembe or pemba. Finding themselves without pemba, the medicine men and women who established themselves in the

Caribbean searched for an alternative; they settled on a concoction they called cascarilla.

Cascarilla is made by gathering hen's eggshells, removing the inner membrane that sticks to the inside of the eggshell, allowing the shells to dry thoroughly, then grinding the shells into a powder, adding some water to the powder so that it becomes a paste, and then putting the paste into little bon bon-like molds so that when it dries it looks like small, white, bon bons. These little cascarilla bon bons are widely available in most botanicas and some New Age shops. If you can't find any, make your own following the directions I just gave. Cascarilla is a perfect uncrossing agent, clarifier of minds, restorer of tired auras, and repellant of evil energies. A little bit in your bathwater is always recommended.

FOUR THIEVES VINEGAR

Legend has it that during the days of the European plague in the 14th century, four thieves who were looting the dead bodies discovered a potion to ward off disease. Although this powerful ingredient is a fairly common item in occult stores and Voodoo shops, it may not be available where you live. Here is the way it is usually made in New Orleans.

Ingredients

- 1 gallon Cider vinegar
- 1oz. Rosemary
- 1 oz. Wormwood
- 1 oz. Lavender
- 1 oz. Rue
- 1 oz. Sage
- 1 oz. Peppermint
- 1 oz. Lemongrass
- 1 oz. Powdered Camphor

Mix everything inside tightly-closed glass container, heat bane Marie (placing container in boiling water) for four minutes each of four days, beginning on a Monday. On the fourth day, strain the solids out and bottle your home-made four thieves vinegar.

WAR WATER

- *Pinch of Iron rust*
- *¼ teaspoon magnetic iron filings*
- *A rusty nail*
- *Fistful of Spanish moss*
- *1 ounce Creosote*

While War Water is mostly associated with cursing, its original intention was actually to strengthen not only one's aura, but one's blood as well. You see, War Water was originally a nutritional supplement meant to supply iron! Add 4 ounces of War Water to your bath once per week to keep your aura strong.

FLYING DEVIL OIL

- *8 ounces olive oil*
- *1 teaspoonful cayenne pepper*
- *13 drops red food coloring*

Although mainly used to curse, Flying Devil can be used to revitalized an extremely lethargic person. Use only a drop every six months.

LOVE OIL

- *8 ounces of extra virgin olive oil*
- *1 ounce gardenia essential oil*

KANANGA WATER

1 ounce oil of ylang ylang
½ ounce oil of neroli
¼ ounce oil of rose
¼ ounce oil of bergamot
16 ounces of alcohol
One grain of musk may be added.

Dilute with distilled water (about a gallon) to
make a toilet water.

8

MY EXPERIENCE WITH THE BLESSED MARIA LIONZA

As a young man of nineteen, I was spending a semester at University of the West Indies in Kingston, Jamaica, where I roomed with a tall Venezuelan Indian named Sancho. We became fast friends and comrades in arms, since he, like me, was a spiritual seeker. In fact, he was destined to become his community's medicine man back in home in Yaracuy state, Venezuela. Towards the end of the semester, Sancho fell deadly ill with what seemed to be a rapidly-spreading cancer. Doctors kept him in hospital and wouldn't allow him to be moved—he, however, wanted desperately to go back to Venezuela. His family did not have the funds to come visit him, he was in school under an Organization of American States scholarship. Not being able to take it anymore, I stole my friend, who now weighed less than a hundred pounds, taking him to a Venezuelan captain of a shrimp boat who said he'd take us both to Venezuela for practically nothing. Miraculously, less than 24 hours later we were in Sancho's house in Yaracuy, near a famous mountain named Sorte, said to be one of the world's centers of spiritual energy. Slipping in and out of a coma on the way home, Sancho now seemed vigorous, standing up on his own.

Although Sancho's father was a medicine man, after examining his son, he understood that Sancho's malady was beyond his grasp. It was decided that Sancho's health would be restored by a shaman named Don Triburcio who lived in a cave near the summit of Sorte mountain. Two of Sancho's strongest brothers carried him as we headed up the mountain. The trail was filled with people; Sorte was a veritable smorgasbord of spiritual practitioners. Literally hundreds made their living there. People from all over Venezuela came to receive help from one of the many healers and quacks who lived in Sorte. After about six hours of arduous, snail-paced climbing, we set camp to rest for the night. Sancho began to fade and I started to become worried. Early the next morning, we continued upward. Sancho appeared to be in much better spirits. At about noon, the sun was blinding me, when I thought I saw a man sitting by the trail. On second look, it was a rock, or so I thought, for the rock turned out to be a diminutive man wearing a reddish brown poncho and a black bowler hat squatting by the side of the trail. The brothers warmly greeted the man, and introduced me as a great friend of Sancho's. Within minutes, we were inside a cave lit by a fire. The man had typically Indian features, copper-toned leather-like skin tautly drawn over prominent cheekbones, dark silver-gray hair pulled back to a short, straight pony tail, and a wide gold-accented, toothy smile that seemed part pleasant, part threatening.

Lario, Sancho's older brother, told me that Don Triburcio was a banco, a master of ceremonies, for Maria Lionza, a local deity said to be a beautiful Indian princess who had lived in the 17th century. Lario said that most of the practitioners in Sorte worshipped Maria Lionza. Don Triburcio also worked with the spirit of Simon Bolivar, legendary liberator of several South American countries. Because Sancho's family was considered very important in their community, Don Triburcio would perform Sancho's healing in private, away from the twenty or so people who had been waiting for hours to see him.

Don Triburcio's assistant, the medium who would actually channel the spirits that would prescribe a cure for Sancho, was a pleasant-looking alabaster-skinned girl named Ramira. "Ramira gets possessed by the *libertador* himself!" Don Triburcio said. "He will cure Sancho today." Looking straight at me, Don Triburcio then said. "But Sancho's sickness is not the reason you're here." Astonished, I didn't know what to say. "Maria Lionza used him to bring you to her."

Sancho laid down next to the fire while his brothers sat near him. A young man began to beat on a drum, while Ramira began to dance around the fire. Another young man sprayed rum on Don Triburcio's naked arms and torso. Don Triburcio then went so near the flames that his arms caught fire! He waved his fiery arms feverishly as the drummer beat a faster beat and Ramira went into a trance. Don Triburcio, his fire put out, then drank something from a gourd and, without warning, he spat whatever it was right into my mouth! I swallowed a horribly acidic substance that made my mouth feel as if it was being pulled in by a vacuum cleaner. I remember experiencing a bout of violent vomiting and losing consciousness. The next thing I remember is waking up in an idyllic pastoral scene with a babbling brook streaming by, two yellow butterflies playfully following each other atop a carpet of pastel-colored wildflowers, and such lush vegetation as I had never seen. From a distance, I saw a silhouette of what appeared to be a person on a squat pony. As the mounted figure approached I noticed that the animal was not a pony, but a tapir, an elephant-like denizen of South America's jungles. His rider was a beautiful young woman covered by a red velvet cape. As she dismounted her unusual beast, she allowed her cape to fall back revealing a perfect nakedness. Although at nineteen I was as interested in the pleasures of the flesh as the next man, the young woman's beauty did not arouse sexual desire in me, but some incomprehensible respect. "Are you the virgin Mary?" I asked.

"No, I am Maria Lionza, and these are my lands." Her voice was indescribably sweet. Her laughter as innocent and clear as spring water. " I've come to tell you about these herbs, Robert." Maria Lionza said. "Pick this romerillo (cinquefoil), and these other herbs and tie them with a string of cotton. Let the water in a pail soak the curative essences out of them, then bathe Sancho with that water that is what will cure the young man!" The other herbs and plants were pennyroyal, patchouli, linden, and mugwort . "After you bathe him thus, clean his skin with a rag wet with camphor, alcohol, and mint." She then said, "And if you want your mother to improve her economic situation, tell her to add sugar, melon juice, rum, and that drink they call Pepsi-Cola to her bathwater!" Maria Lionza spent what seemed like hours teaching me about baths. I then felt very sleepy and drifted into a deep slumber.

A loud shriek from Ramira woke me up. The ceremony was over and Sancho didn't seem to be better. I thought I had experienced a very vivid dream, but then I saw herbs tied by a white cotton string in my hand. I told Don Triburcio what had happened and he immediately prepared a bath for Sancho according to my directions. Within hours Sancho was as good as new.

I don't know exactly what happened to me in that cave. But sincerely believe I was visited by Maria Lionza in some astral plane. The baths she told me about that day have helped hundreds of my friends. Here are some of them.

MARIA LIONZA'S CURATIVE BATH

Try to use fresh herbs whenever possible, but substitute dry ones if necessary. Although no amount is specified, a sprig or small piece of each herb will do.

Ingredients

- Cinquefoil
- Pennyroyal
- Patchouli
- Linden (or tilia)
- Mugwort

- Mint oil
- Alcohol
- Camphor
- A white cotton string.

Put a little bit of camphor and a few drops of mint oil in about 8 ounces of rubbing alcohol, set aside. With a white cotton string, tie up all the herbs. Throw inside a pail and fill pail with water. Allow water to stand a few hours so that the herbs will give the water the essences it needs. Remove herbs, add resulting medicated water to bath, let person needing healing sit or lay down in bathtub, praying that Maria Lionza help him or her. After about twenty minutes, person should be pat-dried and rubbed down with the camphor-alcohol-mint solution. Many maladies are cured after only one application of this procedure. Let at least a day come between procedures, and discontinue if no improvement is seen after three weeks. The herbs of the first bath should be allowed to dry and used in a small red flannel bag as a protective amulet to be carried in one's person.

MARIA LIONZA'S PROSPERITY BATH

Have someone you love, such as your spouse, douse you with sugar, rum, some melon juice (any kind), and the contents of a can of Pepsi, in the name of Maria Lionza. Do the same for the other person. Sit with these ingredients clinging to you for awhile, while envisioning yourself rich. After awhile, take a warm shower to clean yourself. An excellent attracting agent for wealth.

MARIA LIONZA'S LOVE BATH

Add 3 ounces of Florida Water, 1 teaspoon of brown sugar, 3 sticks of cinnamon, a drop of blood from a virgin's menses, and a bit of sperm from a man who has not known woman to your bathwater and the energies raised will make you a magnet for desirable sexual partners. Remember that while in the water you must be thinking sexual thoughts. Works equally well for men and women.

MARIA LIONZA'S ENERGY BATHS

Throw 15 teabags in the tub, add about three gallons of very hot water. Let stand for 10 minutes, fill the tub with warm water, and enjoy!

Another energy-giving bath I learned in Venezuela involved cutting up three limes in quarters, squeezing their juice into a tub with bathwater, then add plenty of rosemary. It really helps!

MARIA LIONZA BATH FOR ACHES AND PAINS

- *1 cup (250g) Epsom salts*
- *1 teaspoon jojoba oil*
- *5-7 drops lavender essential oil*

Add to bathwater; relax for 15 minutes.

9

BATH SALTS, MINERALS, AND OILS

The knowledge and use of aromatics and essential oils for healing and religious purposes goes back to the beginnings of civilization. The ancient Egyptians employed aromatic oils more than 4,000 years ago, and the Greeks and Romans were renowned for their emphasis on the benefits of aromatic bathing.

BATH SALTS (BASIC RECIPE)

The basic bath salt is made out of the following ingredients *(this is enough for five baths)*:

- *3 cups Epsom Salts.*
- *1 cup baking soda.*
- *1 cup sea salt.*

Mix thoroughly with your hands in order to impart mixture with your energy. Separate the mixture into small bowls. Choose the essential oil and the right food coloring for each such as Damiana oil and pink food coloring for a love bath, or Money-drawing oil and green food coloring for a money-drawing bath. Add food coloring a drop at a time until you have the desired color, then, proceed to add the appropriate essential oils. Package and label for later use.

BATH SALT FOR PSYCHIC STRENGTH

To 1 cup of basic recipe bath salt, add the following:
• *3 drops Carnation oil*
• *2 drops Lavender oil*
• *2 drops Rosemary oil*
• *2 drops Basil oil*

Remain in tub for at least half hour, do not do more than once per week.

ANOTHER PSYCHIC STRENGTH BATH

To 1 cup of basic recipe bath salt, add the following:
• *3 drops Lemon Grass oil*
• *2 drops Thyme oil*
• *2 drops Orange oil*
• *1 drop oil of Cloves*
• *1 drop Cinnamon oil*

Use before doing any psychic work

PSYCHIC STRENGTH BATH

To 1 cup of basic recipe bath salt, add the following:
• *Yellow food coloring*
• *3 drops Lavender essential oil*
• *2 drops Rosemary oil*
• *1 drop Peppermint.*
• *1 drop Bergamot.*

Add all ingredients to bathwater, relax in tub for thirty minutes. Do this once per week.

MERLIN BATH SALTS FOR PSYCHIC DEVELOPMENT

To 1 cup of basic recipe bath salt, add the following:
• *8 drops Heliotrope oil*
• *6 drops Violet oil*
• *4 drops Sandalwood*

THIRD EYE BATH SALTS

To 1 cup of basic recipe bath salt, add the following:
• *8 drops Sandalwood oil*
• *3 drops Nutmeg oil*
• *3 drops Cinnamon oil*

MORE BATH SALTS TO OPEN THIRD EYE.

To 1 cup of basic recipe bath salt, add the following:
• *Purple food coloring*
• *4 drops Sandalwood oil*
• *2 drops Myrrh oil*
• *1 drop Frankincense oil*
• *1 drop Cinnamon oil*

Add to warm bathwater, mix thoroughly using your power hand (the one you write with). Remain in tub for at least twenty minutes.

RELAXATION SALTS

To 1 cup of basic recipe bath salt, add the following:
• *Blue or lavender food coloring.*
• *Lilac Essential Oil*

LOVE SALTS

To 1 cup of basic recipe bath salt, add the following:
• *3 drops Peppermint Oil.*
• *2 drops Cinnamon Oil.*
• *2 drops Lemon Oil.*
• *2 drops Almond Extract.*
• *2 drops Vanilla Extract.*

Mix everything, add to your bathwater.

MORE LOVE SALTS

To 1 cup of basic recipe bath salt, add the following:
Pink food coloring
• *3 drops Rosemary oil*
• *2 drops Lavender*
• *1 drop Cardamon oil*
• *1 drop Jasmine oil*

VENUS BATH SALTS TO ATTRACT LOVERS

To 1 cup of basic recipe bath salt, add the following:
• *8 drops Jasmine oil*
• *4 drops Frangipani oil*
• *4 drops Lavender oil*
• *4 drops Rose oil*
• *4 drops Musk oil*

APHRODISIAC BATH SALT

To 1 cup of basic recipe bath salt, add the following:
- *3 drops Sandalwood oil*
- *3 drops Patchouli oil*
- *1 drop Cardamon oil*
- *Red food coloring*

Take this bath before going on a date or before encountering your loved one.

PROSPERITY BATH SALTS

To 1 cup of basic recipe bath salt, add the following:
- *5 drops Cherry oil*
- *2 drops Anise oil*

MONEY BATH SALTS

To 1 cup of basic recipe bath salt, add the following:
- *8 drops Lilac oil*
- *4 drops Violet oil*
- *8 drops Narcissus oil*
- *4 drops Wisteria oil*
- *4 drops Ambergris oil*

EASY LUCK SALTS

To 1 cup of basic recipe bath salt, add the following:
- *Green coloring*
- *Bayberry essential oil (3 drops)*

Add to your bathwater. A bringer of good fortune.

BATH TO RECALL DREAMS

To 1 cup of basic recipe bath salt, add the following:
* *10 Drops Jasmine Oil*
* *6 Drops Lavender Oil*
* *5 Drops Orange Oil*

Mix all ingredients with bathwater, relax in tub, try to recall each dream you've had the last three days.

HEALING BATH SALT

* *2 drops Eucalyptus oil.*
* *1 drop Sandalwood oil*
* *1 ½ cups basic bath salt.*
* *Dark blue food coloring.*

Say Psalm 23 three times while bathing, have a lighted white votive during the bath.

UNCROSSING BATH SALT

To 1 cup of basic recipe bath salt, add the following:
* *3 drops frankincense*
* *3 drops sandalwood*
* *2 drops rosemary*
* *1 drop clove oil*

Splash fresh water over your body after the bath.

PROTECTING FENNEL BATH

To 1 cup of basic recipe bath salt add *9 drops of fennel oil.*
Add to bathwater and say;

> *"callen dan dant, dan dant callen, dant callen dan."*

This incantation makes you immune to curses.

PROTECTION SALTS

To 1 cup of basic recipe bath salt, add the following:
• 3 drops rosemary oil
• 2 drops Frankincense oil.
• 1 drop Lavender oil

Take this bath once per week to keep your aura strong.

PROTECTION WHILE TRAVELLING

Add 1 ounce powdered Comfrey root to your bath salts basic recipe. Add 1/3 of resulting mixture to your bath before traveling, then add 1/3 to your bath while you are away, and save remaining third for just before you return.

ROMAN ENERGIZING MILK SALTS

- *7 oz. Epsom salts*
- *2 oz. powdered milk*
- *2 oz. Borax*
- *2 oz. Sodium Bicarbonate*
- *2 oz. Sea Salt*
- *1 ½ tsp. Glycerin*
- *1 ½ tsp. Vanilla extract*

OATMEAL MILK HEALING BATH

- *4 parts Epsom salts*
- *2 part Sea salt*
- *1 part non fat powdered milk*
- *1 part oatmeal*

Mix all ingredients, add to bathwater.

EGYPTIAN MILK BATH

Curative, psychic-enhancing, good luck bath.

- *½ cup rock salt*
- *1 cup powdered milk.*
- *1 cup Epsom Salts*
- *1 carton buttermilk*
- *1 cup Sea Salt*
- *4 drops Ylang Ylang or Kananga water*
- *3 drops bergamot*
- *2 drops lavender*
- *2 drops peppermint*
- *2 pieces of ginger*
- *3 drops Cedar oil*
- *2 tangerines*
- *2 oranges*

Mix all ingredients in bathwater; cut oranges and tangerines in half and squeeze their juices over your body.

PHOENICIAN MILK BATH FOR STRENGTH

* *1 Cup Cornstarch*
* *2 Cups Dry Milk Powder*
* *2 tsp. of dragon's blood reed.*

Add to bath water. Relax and let the bath do its magic!

USING ESSENTIAL OILS IN BATH SALTS

These are some of the most popular essential oils and their magical qualities. Remember that some of these oils can irritate your skin, so be careful how you use them. Do not use more than ten drops of essential oil per half-cup of bath salts. Use only genuine essential oils.

Acacia - Improves your aura.

Almond - Attracts wealth

Allspice - Strengthens your aura.

Ambergris - Protects against evil and bad luck.

Ambrosia - An aphrodisiac.

Angelica - Associated with the Holy Ghost, it brings peace and harmony to the home.

Avocado - Brings happiness, wealth and long life.

Azalea - Makes you attractive.

Banana - Excites passions.

Bay - A purifying herb.

Bayberry - Brings money to the pockets & blessings to the home.

Benzoin - A cleansing and purifying substance. *[Use only a drop as it can irritate your skin]*

Bergamot - Protects against harm.

Blackberry - Brings money and good luck.

Blue Bonnet - Brings good luck to gamblers.

Calamus - Use when you are trying to dominate another.

Camphor - A legendary psychic protector.

Carnation - Used for gambling luck.

Cedar - Brings good fortune; protects children.

Chamomile - Brings money and love.

Cherry - Add to the bath to cause one to be cheerful and magnetic

Chocolate - An unusual oil that makes friends of enemies.

Chrysanthemum - To increase ones fortitude.

Cinnamon - Used for good luck, money-drawing, and love.

Citronella - Attracts friends to the home, "tricks" to prostitutes, and customers to a place of business.

Civet - Love-drawing.

Clove - An aphrodisiac; also, a psychic enhancer.

Clover - Brings good luck, visions, and ensures that your partner will be loyal to you.

Coconut - I prefer the natural juice to the oil. It is a wonderfu cleanser.

Coffee - Has healing properties when added to the bath water.

Cucumber - Calming effect. Cut in slices and add to bath water.

Cypress - Brings calm and tranquility to hyperactive children. It also opens the third eye and strengthens the psyche.

Dill - Use to cross, it can also uncross with the right incantation, such as *"Elohim, Eloha, Dill. Take this beast away, I will! Give protection to my being, as I will, so mote it be!"*

Dogwood - Keeps evil away.

Eucalyptus - A strong healing oil.

Evergreen - Used by women to turn on men.

Frangipani - An attraction oil, can cause others to tell you their secrets

Frankincense - A sacred oil for anointing and blessing.

Gardenia - A protective oil which will stop others from creating strife in your life. Also a love-drawing oil.

Geranium - An uncrossing oil.

Ginger - A proven aphrodisiac.

Grape - This oil is used for gaining popularity and for money drawing.

Heather - Anoint your purse or wallet with this daily so you will never be without money.

Heliotrope - Protects you from physical harm and also attracts money.

Hemlock - Anti-hex oil.

Hibiscus - Brings wisdom & better concentration.

Hollyberry - Makes women super-desirable.

Honey - Superb aphrodisiac associated with the Yoruba goddess of love, Oshun.

Honeysuckle - Increases your attractiveness and wisdom.

Hyacinth - Attracts love and luck when used in the bath water daily.

Hyssop - A holy oil, it will clean your spirit and draw angelic forces.

Iris - Reputed to make the wearer very attractive, good oil to use when going dancing.

Jasmine - A powerful love oil, used to bind someone to you

Juniper - Wish-granting oil, also used to gain fame.

Lavender - To promote peace in the home and stop gossip, add to bath and mop water.

Leather - Read Psalm 146 as you bathe in water treated with this oil to make you more popular and attract good friends to your life.

Lemon - Used by healers when calling for aid from the spirits, also for drawing love to your life.

Lemongrass - A soothing oil, it also brings love.

Lilac - Improves the memory and promotes sanity and longevity.

Lily - A quieting agent, used when someone is emotionally upset.

Lime - Add 3 drops to bath water along with one drop controlling oil once a week to keep your mate faithful and loyal.

Lotus - Worn by women to make a man generous.

Magnolia - Recommended as an aid in psychic development

Melon - Arouses passions, promotes strength, energy and potency in men.

Mimosa - Induces prophetic dreams when used before going to sleep.

Mistletoe - Attracts customers when used in your place of business.

Morning Glory - Used to protect travelers.

Musk - A love oil whose scent is used to arouse passions and heighten sexual desire.

Myrrh - A powerful guard against any evil force.

Myrtle - Attracts love, Money & good fortune

Narcissus - Used for peaceful sleep and to ward off nightmares.

Nutmeg - Used for removing a jinx from someone, add to bath water. Also used for good luck .

Orange - A highly erotic oil.

Orchid - Aids memory, helps one to focus one's thoughts.

Orris - One of the most potent of love oils. It is also a mighty peace oil.

Papaya - Promotes the acquisition of luxurious items.

Passion Flower - It calms the nerves and brings love to one's life.

Patchouli - An aphrodisiac and psychic enhancer.

Peach - Helps clear the aura, brings peace to the home.

Pennyroyal - An uncrossing oil.

Peony - Brings general good luck, especially for business people.

Peppermint - Psychic enhancer; unhexing; love-drawing oil.

Petunia - Helps you obtain credit.

Pine - A cleansing, purifying scent used in the bath to erase past mistakes and sins.

Pineapple - To bring back a lover, add this oil along with "Come-To-Me" oil to your bath water.

Raspberry - Expectant mothers should start to bathe in water treated with raspberry oil on their sixth month, as this oil helps pregnant women have an easy delivery.

Rose - Attracts affection and love.

Rosemary - A highly respected healing oil.

Rue - Used to protect one from hexes set out by others

Sage - Used for all those who wish to see the future. It also increases wisdom.

Sandalwood - A powerful healing oil, also thought to increase psychic abilities and bring blessings from on high.

Sassafras - Helps win court cases.

Snakeroot - Helps to win the most difficult of court cases.

Spearmint - A protective oil which keeps one's home safe.

Spikenard - A purifying and blessing oil.

Strawberry - Use as an aphrodisiac and good-luck oil.

Sweet Grass - Uplifting oil, helps you forget bad experiences.

Sweet Pea - Promotes loyalty and affection.

Tangerine - A spiritual tonic, use daily in your bath.

Tonka - For luck, love and good health, use in the bath daily.

Tulip - Protects from accidents.

Vanilla - Add to baths and floor washes to bring happiness and peace.

Van Van - Add to bath water if you feel jinxed; a powerful uncrossing oil developed by famed Voodoo queen Marie Laveau in the 19th century.

Verbena - An uncrossing oil.

Vetivert - A powerful anti-hex oil. Overcomes any spell.

Violet - A very strong love oil, use in bath daily to keep you satisfied.

Watermelon - A strong tonic, add to bathwater for extra fortitude.

Wintergreen - Use a few drops in bathwater to keep or induce good health

Wisteria - Attracts good fortune, love, and friendship.

Ylang Ylang - For improved self-esteem; to find a job, also known as kananga.

10

HOME-MADE AND COMMERCIAL PRE-PACKAGED BATHS, CRYSTALS & LOTIONS

PRE-PACKAGED SPIRITUAL BATH BALLS

- *¼ cup baking soda.*
- *2 tablespoons citric acid.*
- *1 tablespoon borax.*
- *2 tablespoons confectioner's sugar.*
- *2 tablespoons almond oil or olive oil.*
- *1 teaspoon vitamin E.*
- *¼ teaspoon essential or perfume oil of your choice.*
- *Food coloring of your choice.*

Mix all dry ingredients, spread on a flat surface. Sprinkle oil and vitamin E on it. Form into balls the size of playing marbles. Let balls dry. Wrap each ball in wax paper. Use by dropping a ball in bathtub, then run warm water on top of it for each bath. A great uncrossing, good luck, and healing bath. Lasts longer if stored in airtight container.

COMMERCIAL BATH CRYSTALS

To use pre-packaged, commercially-prepared scented crystals in spiritual baths, dissolve half the contents of a packet in a tub of water and pour the liquid over yourself as you recite a wish, a prayer, or one of the Psalms. You may also dissolve the crystals in a pail of warm water and use the resulting liquid as a floor wash to rid your home of bad smells and to make your wishes come true.

A sneaky way to use bath crystals is to add some to the rinse water of the laundry of a person you want to influence, for example, surreptitiously adding love crystals to the laundry of a man you want to snatch.. This will dress them—the "victims" of your spells—without their becoming suspicious of your work. If their underwear happens to be in the batch of laundry you tampered with, then you really lucked out, for nothing produces a stronger result than dressing the underwear of a person you want to "hoodoo" in this manner. If you are going for a job interview or out on a date, you can add the appropriate mineral crystals (e.g. Steady Work or Love Me) to your own laundry rinse water and dress yourself.

COLORS AND SPIRITUAL BATHS

In modern times, food coloring has become an important additive to spiritual baths. It is believed that tinting your bath water or bath crystals with a particular color imbues it with the qualities associated with that color. Following I've listed some colors and their associations regarding baths.

Black - Protection; banishing.

Blue - Knowledge; health; change; relaxation of the mind; restful sleep. Protection. Friends.

Brown - Non-human animal energies.

Gold - God; money; strength; the sun.

Gray - Invisibility.

Green - Growth; harmony; renewal. Not to be used by people with cancer, for it promotes growth of everything living, including cancer cells.

Indigo - Deep thoughts; mystical revelations; understanding of higher truths; prophetic dreams.

Orange - Happiness; joy; pleasure; protection; energy.

Pink - Love; sensuality; peace of mind.

Purple - Spiritual meditation; power; healing.

Red - Life; strength; valor. Success in love affairs.

Silver - Goddess; tranquility; the moon.

Violet - Deep visions; inspiration; sobriety.

Turquoise - Confidence building; oratory; helps build immunities.

Yellow - Wisdom, clarity, curiosity, self-esteem. Success in financial matters.

Once you have decided the appropriate coloring for your crystals, the addition of the proper combination of essential oils makes your preparation complete. Here are some effective recipes:

COURT VICTORY BATH CRYSTALS

Add the following combination of ingredients to your pre-made crystals (p. 63):
- *Court Case Powder*
- *¼ oz. Almond Oil*
- *¼ oz. Anise Oil*
- *¼ oz. Pine Oil*
- *¼ oz. Angelica Oil*
- *Blue coloring*

HEALING BATH CRYSTALS

Add the following combination of ingredients to your pre-made crystals (p. 63):
- *¼ oz. Coconut Oil*
- *¼ oz. Sage Oil*
- *¼ oz. Myrrh Oil*
- *¼ oz. Cedar Oil*
- *Red coloring*

LUCKY LOTTERY BATH CRYSTALS

Add the following combination of ingredients to your pre-made crystals (p. 63):
- *¼ oz. Allspice Oil*
- *¼ oz. Sage Oil*
- *¼ oz. Clover Oil*
- *¼ oz. Cedarwood Oil*
- *Green coloring*

PROPHECY BATH CRYSTALS

Add the following combination of ingredients to your pre-made crystals [p. 63]:
- ¼ oz. Acacia Oil
- ¼ oz. Coconut Oil
- ¼ oz. Peppermint Oil
- ¼ oz. Frankincense Oil
- Purple coloring

LOVE BATH CRYSTALS

Add the following combination of ingredients to your pre-made crystals [p. 63]:
- ¼ oz. Cinamon Oil
- ¼ oz. Lilac Oil
- ¼ oz. Honey Oil
- ¼ oz. Ambergris Oil
- Red coloring

MONEY DRAWING BATH CRYSTALS

Add the following combination of ingredients to your pre-made crystals [p. 63]:
- ¼ oz. Spearmint Oil
- ¼ oz. Peppermint Oil
- ¼ oz. Coconut Oil
- ¼ oz. Sassafras Oil
- ¼ oz. Anise Oil
- Green coloring

SUCCESS BATH CRYSTALS

Add the following combination of ingredients to your pre-made crystals [p. 63]:
- ¼ oz. Coconut Oil
- ¼ oz. Nutmeg Oil
- ¼ oz. Heather Oil
- ¼ oz. Mint Oil
- Yellow coloring

SPELL-BREAKING BATH CRYSTALS

Add the following combination of ingredients to your pre-made crystals [p. 63]:
- ¼ oz. Sandalwood Oil
- ¼ oz. Myrrh Oil
- ¼ oz. Lilac Oil
- ¼ oz. Anise Oil
- Black coloring

MAKE YOUR OWN BODY LOTIONS

Body lotions are a great way to enhance the effects of your baths. Apply your homemade lotion after your daily bath to reinforce the beneficial effects of your ritual. The same combination of essential oils used to create your bath crystals or those used in your bath water can be added to unscented cold cream or body lotion.

GO AWAY EVIL BODY LOTION

Mix the following ingredients in a bowl and store in a sealed jar until ready for use.
- *1 cup unscented cold cream or body lotion*
- *¼ oz. Dragon Blood Oil*
- *¼ oz. Peppermint Oil*
- *¼ oz. Angelica Oil*
- *¼ oz. Mistletoe Oil*

PURIFICATION BODY LOTION

Mix the following ingredients in a bowl and store in a sealed jar until ready for use.
- *1 cup unscented cold cream or body lotion*
- *¼ oz. Coconut Oil*
- *¼ oz. Sage Oil*
- *¼ oz. Eucalyptus Oil*
- *¼ oz. Aster Oil*

MONEY DRAWING BODY LOTION

Mix the following ingredients in a bowl and store in a sealed jar until ready for use.
- *1 cup unscented cold cream or body lotion*
- *¼ oz. Almond Oil*
- *¼ oz. Bayberry Oil*
- *¼ oz. Mint Oil*
- *¼ oz. Vervain Oil*

PSYCHIC POWER BODY LOTION

Mix the following ingredients in a bowl and store in a sealed jar until ready for use.
- *1 cup unscented cold cream or body lotion*
- *¼ oz. Acacia Oil*
- *¼ oz. Anise Oil*
- *¼ oz. Sandalwood Oil*
- *¼ oz. Lilac Oil*

LUCK BODY LOTION

Mix the following ingredients in a bowl and store in a sealed jar until ready for use.
- *1 cup unscented cold cream or body lotion*
- *¼ oz. Cinnamon Oil*
- *¼ oz. Cypress Oil*
- *¼ oz. Lotus Oil*

BODY LOTION TO ATTRACT WOMEN

Mix the following ingredients in a bowl and store in a sealed jar until ready for use.
- *1 cup unscented cold cream or body lotion*
- *¼ oz. Bay Oil*
- *¼ oz. Musk Oil*
- *¼ oz. Patchouly Oil*
- *¼ oz. Violet Oil*

BODY LOTION TO ATTRACT MEN

Mix the following ingredients in a bowl and store in a sealed jar until ready for use.
- *1 cup unscented cold cream or body lotion*
- *¼ oz. Jasmine Oil*
- *¼ oz. Gardenia Oil*
- *¼ oz. Lavender Oil*
- *¼ oz. Musk Oil*

PROTECTION BODY LOTION

Mix the following ingredients in a bowl and store in a sealed jar until ready for use.
- *1 cup unscented cold cream or body lotion*
- *¼ oz. Cypress Oil*
- *¼ oz. Myrrh Oil*
- *¼ oz. Violet Oil*
- *¼ oz. Rosemary Oil*

HEX-BREAKING BODY LOTION

Mix the following ingredients in a bowl and store in a sealed jar until ready for use.
- *1 cup unscented cold cream or body lotion*
- *¼ oz. Bergamot Oil*
- *¼ oz. Rue Oil*
- *¼ oz. Rosemary Oil*
- *¼ oz. Vertivert Oil*

MEDITATION BODY LOTION

Mix the following ingredients in a bowl and store in a sealed jar until ready for use.
- *1 cup unscented cold cream or body lotion*
- *¼ oz. Acacia Oil*
- *¼ oz. Jasmine Oil*
- *¼ oz. Nutmeg Oil*
- *¼ oz. Magnolia Oil*

11

BATHS ACROSS CULTURES

JUDAISM: THE MIKVEH

According to Jewish tradition, a mikveh, or ritual bath for women, is constructed before any other part of a synagogue. A typical modern mikveh is made out of tile, resembling a Jacuzzi without jets. It has the capacity to hold 40 sa'ahs (about 185 gallons) of Mayim Chaim, or "living water" collected in a rooftop cistern or as natural ice. In Judaism, the number 40 is rich in associations: a person spends 40 weeks in utero, the Great Flood lasted 40 days, and the Israelites wandered the desert for 40 years.

The act of ritual immersion in water carries strong associations in Judeo-Christian traditions. It makes it possible for women to be free of sins so they can serve as carriers of new lives, the vital function of the mikveh, which John the Baptist transformed into an even more powerful symbol, baptism, the shedding off of one's old life to emerge into a new, clean existence. A woman walks down the steps of the mikveh into chest-high water as the Shomeret (trained attendant) sees that her whole body is immersed, puts a special cloth on her head when she stands, and listens as the bather recites a prayer. The number of dips and the prayers vary.

CHRISTIANITY: BAPTISM

Although many Christian denominations have modified the original baptism by total immersion to a simple sprinkling of water on the head, many others retain the custom. Rural Fundamentalist Christians in the United States will go to natural bodies of water to practice the sacrament of baptism. The Bible states that Jesus was baptized by his cousin John, son of Zakariah, by total immersion in the waters of the river Jordan. To a Christian, baptism is the most important sacrament. This ritual bath identifies the person as a member of Christ's Church. It also signifies the leaving behind of sins and wickedness and the rising to a new life in Jesus.

HINDUISM: MATA GANGA: ABISHEKA

Certain rivers in India are thought to be so sacred that they are believed to be gods and goddesses. Chief among these is the Ganges, called Mother Ganges ("Mata Ganga" in Sanskrit). So sacred are the waters of this river that many of the pious believe that to die by its shore assures one of liberation from re-birth. Less dramatic is the ritual of abisheka, where a priest in a temple sprinkles water on the temple-goers as a sign of blessing. Also, during Diwali, the Hindu festival of lights, the pious get up before dawn to take an oil bath, signifying the cleansing of evil thoughts and deeds and the beginning of a new life.

JAVANESE TRADITIONS: MITONI

Ritual bathing is very important in Java, where people normally bathe several times a day. The mitoni is a ritual bathing of a husband and wife done when the wife is seven months pregnant with the couple's first child. The couple sits on two chairs while different authority figures, such as a priest and the couple's grandparents ritually

Bathe the husband and wife, reciting incantations so that they may have a healthy baby and their future will be bright and free of sorrow.

ISLAM: THE HAMMAM

Although hammams mainly serve the function of "regular" Turkish baths, these public places were sometimes thought of as inhabited by djinn and other spiritual beings who helped bathers overcome spiritual maladies. The hammam was also thought to possess medicinal qualities; in fact, Caliph al'Qu'imin, writing in A.D.1032, said that "The hammam cured small pox and other hidden illnesses." After centuries of healing, the hammam has picked up the nickname "silent doctor" from Muslims. Although not as important as it used to be, Hammams are to be found in Turkey and throughout the Muslim world.

HOODOO

Herbal baths, mineral bath crystals, and floor washes have been a part of the African-American traditions known as root medicine and Hoodoo for a very long time. Generally speaking, these practices contain elements of African and European magical traditions as well as some Native American plant lore .

Since the early part of the 20th century, mineral salts, liquid detergents, room sprays, and other modern bathing and cleaning supplies have been manufactured in convenient forms for use in magical cleansing and purification rites. Modern manufacturers catering to the Hoodoo trade package baths such as Peaceful Home Bath and Floor Wash Crystals, Crown of Success Crystals and Oil, etc.

In Hoodoo, bathing a set number of times or washing down the walls, floors, and doorstep of one's home or place of business in a ritual manner is part of one's daily religious duties. Generally, the disposal of used bath water or floor wash from such work consists of throwing it to the east at sunrise while saying a prayer, Psalm, or incantation. Sometimes the used bathwater is saved to be later added to floor and wall washes.

SUB-SAHARAN AFRICA

In The Gambia, a crocodile-infested pool of water called Katchikally is one of the country's leading attractions. The waters of the pool are thought to be holy. The crocodiles in the pool are tame and feed only on fish. Many miracles are reported each year at the site.

FOOTNOTES

[1] According to ancient Jewish laws of family purity, women must refrain from sex until they have ritually immersed themselves — before marriage, following childbirth, and seven days after menstruation ends. A community must build a mikveh before a synagogue: prayers can be offered wherever ten men gather, but there can be no marital relations without a mikveh..

[2] In the Hoodoo tradition, some recipes call for water left over after you bathe, but this is not usually advisable as that water may contain negative energies

[3] In some cases, especially involving baths from the Santería tradition, the head should not be wet.

CONCLUSION

Perhaps no action one can take to protect ones self against negativity, psychic attacks, or bad luck is as intimate as the bath. Clothed only by water, with our nakedness reminding us both of the wonder of birth and the vulnerability of our material bodies, the bath is the ultimate psychic cleanser. In this book I have delved into many ways of using the bath as a stalwart of protection, as the line of first defense against psychic attacks. I have gone deeper and wider than any writer before me in giving you, the reader, a myriad options. The techniques I've described run the gamut from simple water-only cleansings to complicated treatments involving multiple steps and many ingredients. Everyone can find a technique here appropriate to the particular circumstance being encountered by that person.

The important thing to remember is that no matter how efficacious the technique employed has proven to be in the past, it is ultimately the attitude, focus, and determination you bring to the bath which will make it work. I give you the ammunition, but you must provide the weapon and the aim, so take aim against that which is assailing your senses and, with the purity of the bath, eliminate it from your existence forever. Water is the nearest physical metaphor we have for life itself; the one common thread uniting all the baths I mention here is water, thus you can see the symbolic significance that these techniques intrinsically hold: We are using LIFE (WATER) to fight evil. We are bringing LIFE (WATER) to our spirits through specific rituals designed to cover our physical bodies with LIFE (WATER) itself! As you make use of water in dissolving whatever it is that stands between you and happiness, remember that there is no more potent universal solvent. Approach each action you learn from this book with faith and devotion, perform each bath with a single-minded resolve not to allow anything to stand in the way of your self-realization. Do this, and everything else will fall into place. May the Divine Forces that inspired these baths be with you now and always to guard and protect your efforts, So Be It!

ABOUT THE AUTHOR

I am an Accompong Maroon. The Maroon settlement of Accompong is perched high up in the mountains of St. Elizabeth in western Jamaica, bordering the western parishes of St. James and Trelawny. This state is a nation within the nation of the island of Jamaica. Its citizens are descendants of former runaway slaves who fled the slave plantations of Jamaica to form their own communities. They live on lands granted under a treaty and continue to practice and enjoy the traditional customs handed down to them by their African guerilla forefathers. Accompong was a supply base for the Maroons during their war for freedom against the British from 1655 until the signing of the Peace Treaty between both parties on March 1st, 1739. The hero of Accompong was Kojo, who led its armies during those war years and never lost a battle. Since January 6, 1738, when Kojo routed the British army and slaughtered every member within it except one, Accompong has never again had a battle on its soil. He requested the one remaining English general to take a message to the then governor Edward Trelawny that the British should send more soldiers, as the Maroons were ready to repeat their feat. There have been no murders in the community for hundreds of years since.

On my mothers side I am a direct descendant of Kojo. My mother, Princess Elena Kojo, is one eighth African, one eighth English and the rest Arawak Indian. My father, Joseph Al Rumi, was a Coptic Christian priest from Egypt sent to instruct a Rastafarian community in the 1940's. He fell in love with my mother and joined her in Accompong, where he died in the fate 50's. After my fathers death, I lived in Egypt in a Coptic community where first learned that I was meant to be a practitioner. My first teacher was my grandmother, Miriam A! Rumia. From Egypt I traveled through Africa, studying astrology with the Dogon and Ifa divination with the Yoruba. I went back to Jamaica after twenty years in 1980 when my brother was elected Colonel of Accompong. In 1985 I went to Sorte Mountain in Venezuela to learn about Maria Lionza, then I studied Theology and Religious Studies at the University of the West Indies, where I obtained my Ph.D. in 1992. A revelation I received in October of 1992 forced me to use the name Robert Laremy from then on. Since then I have been deeply involved with the study of Kabbalah and with recording the mystical practices of my Coptic ancestors. I enjoy anonymity and shun most people except to help them. I believe in empowering people, thus I have begun to publish practical guides to spiritual enlightenment and self-defense such as The Psalm Workbook, Spiritual Cleansing and Psychic Defenses, and Original Publications' Complete Bath Book. I choose to keep my present whereabouts private, but can always be reached for questions through my publishers. Peace and Light to All of You!

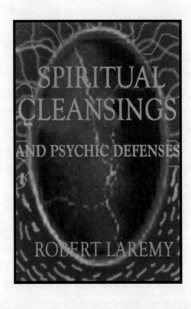

SPIRITUAL CLEANSINGS & PSYCHIC DEFENSES

By Robert Laremy

Psychic attacks are real and their effects can be devastating to the victim. Negative vibrations can be as harmful as bacteria, germs and viruses. There are time-honored methods of fighting these insidious and pernicious agents of distress. These techniques are described in this book and they can be applied by you. No special training or supernatural powers are needed to successfully employ these remedies. All of the procedures described in this book are safe and effective, follow the instructions without the slightest deviation. The cleansings provided are intended as *"over-the-counter"* prescriptions to be used by anyone being victimized by these agents of chaos.

ISBN 0-942272-72-2 5½"x 8½" 112 pages $9.95

Item #222
$11.95

THE PSALM WORKBOOK

by Robert Laremy

Work with the Psalms to
Empower, Enrich and Enhance Your Life!

This LARGE PRINT King James version of the Book of Psalms contains nearly 400 simple rituals and procedures that can be used to help you accomplish anything you desire. Use the situational index provided to decide which psalm to pray for your specific need.

Peace, Protection, Health,
Success, Money, Love,
Faith, Inspiration, Spiritual Strength
And much more!

Approach your worship with a clean heart and a child-like faith in God's infinite wisdom and you will derive tremendous results from the powers of the psalms.

UNHEXING AND JINX REMOVING

BY DONNA ROSE

Everywhere we turn these days it seems as if there are forces working against us. You don't need to spend your time thinking, worrying about or stressing over the evils that are constantly prowling. Cast out all forces of negativity, evil thoughts, evil intentions, evil spirits and so on. Break up conspiracies, dispel rumors, blanket your enemies with suffering and confusion. Believe it or not there are ways to protect yourself in this modern world. The easy to perform rituals and spells provided in this book will allow you to escape the dangers hounding you.

ISBN 0-942272-84-6 5½"x 8½" $6.95

ITEM #224
$6.95

Revised and Expanded

Success and Power Through Psalms

By Donna Rose

For thousands of years, men and women have found in the Psalms the perfect prayer book, possessing wisdom applicable to every human situation. Wise men and women of deep mystical insight have also learned to decipher the magical formulas David and the other Psalmists hid behind the written words. These formulas help the seeker solve everyday problems, achieve higher states of consciousness, gain material and spiritual wealth, as well as help defend himself or herself against psychic attacks and all manner of dangers.

The Revised and Expanded edition of Donna Rose's classic offers over 300 simple to perform magical rituals to help you manifest all of your desires using the magical powers of the psalms.

ISBN 0-942272-79-X 5½"x 8½ $6.95

TOLL FREE: 1 (888) OCCULT - 1   **WWW.OCCULT1.COM**

HELPING YOURSELF WITH SELECTED PRAYERS
-VOLUME 2-
OVER 170 PRAYERS!

The prayers from Volume 2 come from diverse sources. Most originated in Roman Catholicism and can still be found in one form or another on the reverse of little pocket pictures of saints, or in collections of popular prayers. Another source for these prayers is the French Spiritist movement begun in the 1800's by Allan Kardec, which has become a force in Latin America under the name Espiritismo. The third source, representing perhaps the most mystical, magical, and practical aspects of these prayers, is found among the indigenous populations where Santería has taken root.

These prayers will provide a foundation upon which you can build your faith and beliefs. It is through this faith that your prayers will be fulfilled. The devotions within these pages will help you pray consciously, vigorously, sincerely and honestly. True prayer can only come from within yourself.